Indian
MYTHOLOGY

Other titles in the *World Mythology* series include:

Chinese Mythology

Egyptian Mythology

Greek Mythology

Roman Mythology

WORLD
MYTHOLOGY

Indian
MYTHOLOGY

Don Nardo

ReferencePoint
Press

San Diego, CA

© 2021 ReferencePoint Press, Inc.
Printed in the United States

For more information, contact:
ReferencePoint Press, Inc.
PO Box 27779
San Diego, CA 92198
www.ReferencePointPress.com

LIBRARY OF CONGRESS CATALOGING-IN-PUBLICATION DATA

Name: Nardo, Don, 1947– author.
Title: Indian Mythology/Don Nardo.
Description: San Diego, CA: ReferencePoint Press, 2020. | Series: World
    Mythology | Includes bibliographical references and index.
Identifiers: LCCN 2019051372 (print) | LCCN 2019051373 (ebook) | ISBN
    9781682828151 (library binding) | ISBN 9781682828168 (ebook)
Subjects: LCSH: Mythology, Indic. | Hindu mythology. | CYAC: Mythology,
    Indic. | Hindu mythology.
Classification: LCC BL2003 .N38 2020 (print) | LCC BL2003 (ebook) | DDC
    294.5/13–dc23
LC record available at https://lccn.loc.gov/2019051372
LC ebook record available at https://lccn.loc.gov/2019051373

CONTENTS

KEY HINDU GODS

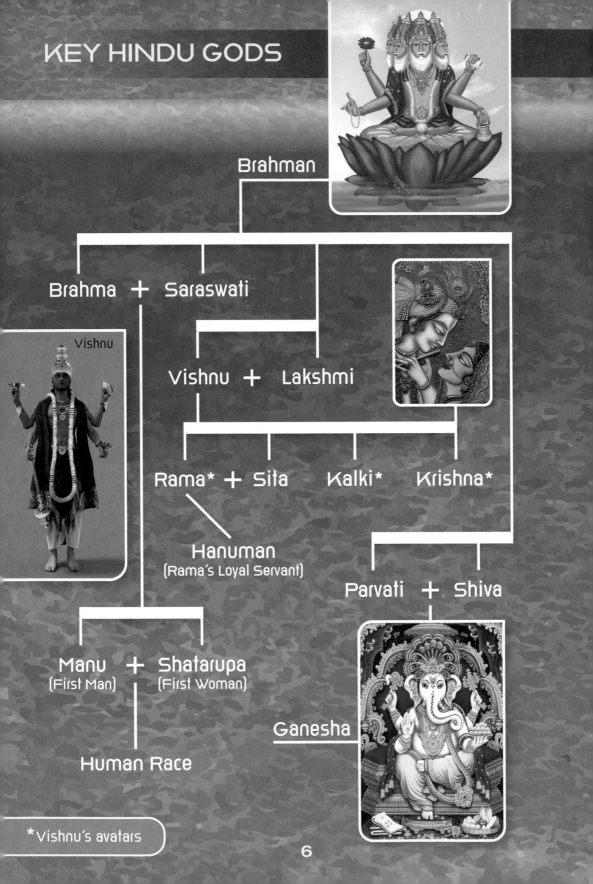

Brahman

Brahma + **Saraswati**

Vishnu

Vishnu + **Lakshmi**

Rama* + **Sita**   **Kalki***   **Krishna***

Hanuman
(Rama's Loyal Servant)

Parvati + **Shiva**

Manu + **Shatarupa**
(First Man)   (First Woman)

Ganesha

Human Race

*Vishnu's avatars

Mighty Indra Versus the Evil Demon

According to a widely popular Hindu myth, a very long time ago, when humanity was still young, most of India's inhabitants were farmers. They did their best to scratch out meager livings from the land, which, of course, required sufficient rains to water their crops. At times this was exceedingly difficult because of a dreaded demon named Vritra. He lived in clouds, where he relentlessly absorbed moisture, thereby severely reducing rainfall. In fact, when Vritra visited a given region for a while, that area suffered from a drought that devastated crops and brought widespread hunger to the locals.

> **PRITHIVI**
> An early Indian earth goddess who married the sky god Dyaus

There seemed to be no way to stop Vritra's reign of skyborne terror. The farmers frequently prayed to the earth goddess Prithivi and the sky god Dyaus, begging those deities to confront and stop the demon. But Vritra was a good deal stronger than either Prithivi or Dyaus, and neither of them dared to tangle with him.

Mortal Combat in the Sky

Fortunately for the farmers, the situation was not as hopeless as it seemed. One day Prithivi noticed an unusual twinge of pain in her abdomen and soon, to her surprise, she had given birth to a new god. It was clear that there was something special about him: when he emerged from Prithivi's womb, the ground, mountains, and plains all trembled as if a great earthquake were about to strike. This sign did prove prophetic because the child—Indra by name—rapidly grew into a strong, highly energetic being. He swiftly learned to fight with an array of weapons and to drive a speeding chariot.

INDRA
The son of Prithivi and Dyaus and the chief early Indian god

He feared nothing and no one—and that included the cloud demon, Vritra. In fact, Indra announced that he intended to rid the world of that loathsome being. It appeared, Indra said, that he was the only one who could eliminate the menace that was robbing humans of the precious water they required to sustain themselves. Grabbing the thunderbolt he had taught himself to use as a weapon, he leapt onto his chariot and charged forth to engage the demon in mortal combat.

When the farmers and other villagers in the countryside saw the young god riding his chariot at top speed, they realized that he must be coming to their rescue. They cheered him on and raised their voices in a hymn meant to encourage him. "Mighty is Indra!" they cried out in unison. "Greatness be his, the Thunderer. Wide as the heaven extends his power!"[1]

Wasting little time, the young deity raced toward the huge cloud in which Vritra was then residing. The demon, who had not yet heard of Indra, demanded to know who dared to intrude into his domain. Indra replied that it was the proud son of Prithivi and Dyaus who dared. Furthermore, said the god, Vritra should prepare to be erased from existence.

At first, the demon merely smiled, for he was at least ten times larger than Indra and considered himself invincible. But Vritra's smug look quickly disappeared as Indra drove his stout chariot right at his monstrous opponent. The determined attacker "maimed Vritra by chopping off his right arm," according to the account in the much-revered ancient Indian document, the Mahabharata. "He ripped Vritra's belly open and issuing forth went to the nearby beach. And directing his thunderbolt at the water hurled it so that the surf flew and hit Vritra."[2] The white-hot thunderbolt emerged from that flying wave and struck the demon's midsection hard, making him suddenly shudder in pain. The weapon speedily penetrated the creature's body, frying its heart, lungs, and other vital organs.

Seconds later, Vritra was dead, and the torrents of water trapped in his enormous body burst outward and quickly filled streams and lakes all across India and well beyond. At that

The primeval chief god Indra, who was born from the divine womb of the earth goddess Prithivi, rides his trusty sacred elephant Airavata in this early modern Indian painting.

moment, Indra detected an unusual sound. It took him only a moment to realize that it was the clamor of millions of human voices singing a hymn of thanks in his honor.

Order and Chaos: The Eternal Struggle

Analyzed in its most basic form, the heroic tale of Indra's destruction of the cloud demon is a potent example of a myth in which good confronts and overcomes evil. In fact, the age-old theme of good triumphing over evil is common in Hindu mythology. According to Jayaram V, a leading Indian expert on Hinduism,

> Hinduism clearly identifies the difference between good and evil (dharma and adharma). According to several of the Hindu scriptures, God stands between order and chaos, or figuratively between good and evil. Existence is defined by a constant struggle between order and chaos or between good and evil. The gods, who are incapable of error and evil, are collectively called the *devas*. They represent the force of good that exists in a variety of forms throughout the universe. The demons, or *asuras*, represent evil, another potent force that always remains a threat to the universal order.[3]

Numerous Hindu myths, like the one in which Indra slays Vritra, describe fights between the *devas* and *asuras*. Such battles are in a sense built into Hinduism and its mythology, much as the constant tensions between God and the devil exist in Christian lore. In fact, just as the devil is often said to be a fallen angel, some Indian myths claim that the evil *asuras* started as good *devas* and at some point crossed over to the dark side. In whatever manner the eternal struggle between order and chaos emerged, it lies at the heart of many religions, and Hinduism, with its numerous attending myths, is no exception.

CHAPTER ONE

The Ancient Indians and Their Gods

India possesses one of the world's richest and most complex mythologies. It is essentially a vast collection of tales associated with Hinduism, which is India's oldest and primary religion. The third-largest faith, next to Christianity and Islam, Hinduism spawned its myths in ancient times, and over the ensuing centuries these stories retained their religious and social impact. As noted modern mythologist Veronica Ions explains, Hindu mythology "is distinguished from that of most other lands, and certainly from those of the West, by the fact that it is still part of a living culture—and not merely of the uneducated masses, but of every level of society."[4]

Indeed, many Hindu myths are regular features of modern Indian life. One prominent example occurs each October or November in the large-scale religious festival of Diwali. It celebrates the principal myth of Lakshmi, the goddess of wealth and good fortune. In that story, back at the beginning of time she held the seed of divine desire in her hand. By releasing it, she unleashed nature's dynamic forces, making the creation of the world by other gods possible. "All over India," writes scholar Shahrukh Husain, "hundreds of little oil lamps are lighted and placed around houses and roof-tops and even floated on ponds and streams to attract

Lakshmi, the Hindu goddess of wealth, light, good fortune, wisdom, and fertility, pictured here, was said to have released the seed of divine desire, making the creation of the world possible.

her to them. The whole of India is like a fairyland, glittering and twinkling in devotion to this lovable goddess who never stays with anyone for long but is an eternal wanderer."[5]

Deep Roots in the Indus Valley

Thus, Indian mythology is not only a living, breathing literary corpus, or group of stories, but also a central feature of Hinduism. The stories and the faith developed side by side over the course of thousands of years. The precise beginnings and sources of those stories are lost in the cloudy mists of time. But experts have managed to piece together a rough picture of their origins.

Some thirty-five hundred years ago the broad valley of the Indus River, located in what was then northwest India (but today is Pakistan), was home to India's earliest civilization. Modern historians dubbed it the Harappan culture. Arising between 3000 and 2600 BCE, the Harappans erected numerous cities and towns, some with populations of fifty thousand or more. They dwelled in well-built brick homes that lined streets forming modern-looking grids, and they carried on intensive trade with areas as distant as Mesopotamia (now Iraq).

No one yet knows exactly why, but during the two or so centuries following 1900 BCE, the Harappans slowly but steadily abandoned their well-organized cities. Thereafter, their descendants occupied small villages scattered throughout the Indus Valley. While these population movements were happening, substantial cultural changes occurred as well. The end result was that the former Harappan culture gradually morphed into a new civilization that historians call the Vedic culture.

The Emergence of the Vedas

One of the major changes that occurred in the transition from Harappan to Vedic culture was literary in nature. Early Vedic priests and scribes got rid of the old Harappan writing system and began using an early rendition of Sanskrit. The reason for this change is not completely understood. But it could be that Harappan script and vocabulary were not flexible enough to express the complex literary ideas that inspired the Vedic writers. In contrast, Sanskrit is a highly expressive language that is well suited to producing literature, including written versions of myths.

Many of these Vedic writings have survived intact, and they provide valuable insights into early Hindu beliefs and the many legends about the gods and their exploits. Among the more crucial Vedic documents are the Vedas. The names of their authors are unknown, but experts think they were priests, poets, philosophers, and other members of the small, well-to-do Vedic educated class. These intellectuals did not need to work for a living, so they had the time to speculate, discuss, and write about the nature of the universe and the meaning of life. In the words of religious studies scholar Karel Werner, to convey those ideas from the Vedas to ordinary folk who could not read, they fashioned public religious ceremonies that average people could watch or take part in. These ceremonies included "re-enactments of the drama of creation and of the struggle between the forces of life and stagnation or decay through the use of symbolic rituals, both private and communal."[6] Through such religious festivals, individual families and entire communities learned about the gods and myths discussed in detail in the Vedas.

The oldest and most renowned of those works is the *Rig-Veda*, meaning "Rich in Knowledge." It was written sometime between 1500 and 1200 BCE and features ten parts. Traditionally called books, each is composed of prayers and hymns to various Vedic deities. Three other Vedas—the *Sama-Veda*, *Yajur-Veda*, and *Atharva-Veda*, which also feature hymns to divine beings—emerged a bit later than the *Rig-Veda*.

Early Vedic Deities and Rituals

Several of the Vedic hymns mention assorted aspects of daily life. By studying them, therefore, modern scholars have learned a fair amount about Vedic society. This includes the religious system and its numerous gods. A large proportion of those deities were associated with natural objects and forces such as the sun, moon, sky, fire, wind, storms, thunder, earthquakes, and so forth.

VARUNA
Once the chief god, but in later Hindu lore a lesser deity of lakes and rivers

According to the myths recounted in the hymns, over time there had been more than one change of leadership among the gods. The original chief of the divine pantheon appears to have been the sky deity Dyaus, the mate of the earth goddess Prithivi. For reasons that remain unclear, at some point Dyaus underwent a demotion in status, and his eldest son, Varuna, became the leader of the gods. A sky god like his father, Varuna was also the lord of the underworld, where human spirits dwelled after death. In addition, he served as overseer of law and order as well as the bringer of rain. A Vedic hymn to Varuna contains this

How Ganesha Lost His Tusk

The elephant-headed deity Ganesha—the god of wisdom, arts, learning, and beginnings—is usually depicted with one broken tusk. Of the many myths that explain how he lost it, one describes Ganesha as having a stomachache from eating too many of the sweets he is well-known for enjoying. Hoping to make himself feel better, he rode his giant mouse into the forest to enjoy the wonders of nature. There, a large snake appeared and frightened the mouse, causing Ganesha to fall to the ground. The impact of the fall made the god's protruding belly burst open, and some of the sweets he had eaten fell out. Calmly, the even-tempered elephant-headed divinity placed the sweets back in his belly and then, to ensure that they remained there, he picked up the snake and wrapped it around his belly like a belt. At that moment, the moon, who had witnessed the incident, began to laugh, which irritated Ganesha. To teach the moon to be more polite, the god broke off one of his tusks and tossed it at the silvery orb of night. When the tusk hit its mark, the moon withdrew its light momentarily, making the night completely black. But after a while it began to shine once more. Meanwhile, Ganesha thereafter had only one tusk.

prayer designed to get his attention: "I saw his car [chariot] above the earth. He has accepted these my songs. Varuna, hear this call of mine. Be gracious unto us this day, longing for help I cried to you. You, o wise God, are Lord of all, you are the King of earth and heaven. Hear, as you go on your way."[7]

In time, as had happened to his father, Varuna diminished in rank, and the role of chief god was taken over by his brother, Indra. Some modern experts suspect that this change was related to the mythical reign of terror perpetrated by the awful demon Vritra. The fact that the myths say Indra—and not Varuna—killed the demon, may indicate that for some reason Varuna lacked the fortitude to do so, and Indra's victory over Vritra allowed him to supplant his brother as divine leader. For whatever reason that Indra achieved that lofty position, he remained the chief divinity for the rest of the Vedic age (circa 1500–500 BCE).

This eighteenth-century Indian rendering shows the powerful sky god Varuna riding the sea monster Makara. In time, according to various myths, Varuna was demoted in status and replaced as chief god by Indra.

Indians of that era did not worship Varuna, Indra, and the other Vedic gods in temples; these structures did not appear in India until centuries later. Instead, Vedic believers erected outdoor brick or stone altars on which they enacted *agni yagas*, or fire sacrifices. Priests led the rituals, during which worshippers lit sacred fires and chanted hymns, including those written down in the

Vedas. This facet of worship, which later became important in Hinduism, honored any and all Vedic gods. But regardless of

which deity was the focus of a hymn or prayer, in Vedic times the fire god, Agni, was also present in the form of the sacred flames. Ions explains:

> He is kindled by the hand not only of priests, when he becomes the sacrificial fire, but also by the hand of every person, whom he warms, protects, and nourishes in the form of the hearth fire. The smoke from these earthly fires rises again to become the clouds of the atmosphere. Omnipresent in the universe, Agni touches and observes every aspect, however mundane, of human life.[8]

From Vedic to Hindu

The gods, rituals, myths, and other elements of the Vedic religion are considered to be the initial basis for the early Hindu faith. That faith matured a little at a time but reached its approximate modern form by about 1500 CE.

Particularly important in the steady transition from the Vedic faith to Hinduism was a general reordering of and fresh way of looking at the principal gods. Indeed, some of those divinities underwent fairly substantial changes. Perhaps the best-known example is the leading Vedic deity, Indra. During the Vedic centuries, he was seen as a dominant war god who could control thunder, lightning, and other aspects of the weather, much like the ancient Greek god Zeus. As classical Hinduism arose, however, Indra became a minor deity associated mainly with destructive rainstorms.

The Hindu religion and mythology did not replace Indra with a single foremost god. Instead, several deities assumed major importance and were seen as more or less equal in influence and status. Chief among them were a creator god, Brahma; a sort of overall protector deity named Vishnu; and Shiva, whose task was to eradicate the world's wasteful aspects and replace them with more constructive ones.

As Hinduism developed in its classical age, it also placed special emphasis on several other Vedic gods, often assigning them different attributes or increased or decreased prominence than in the past. Mitra, for instance, had been an overseer of contracts in Vedic times; as a Hindu deity, however, he became associated with the rising sun and took the role of god of friendship. The fire god, Agni, meanwhile, also transitioned from the Vedic religion to Hinduism, but with diminished prestige. From a central position in all sacrifices, he devolved into a far less impressive keeper of knowledge and witness to human rites of passage. Similarly, the once mighty Varuna became a mere supervisor of lakes, rivers, and other waterways.

Early Hinduism also introduced some new deities. Among the better-known examples was Ganesha, the god of wisdom and the fine arts, who first appeared sometime during the second century CE. Envisioned as a man with an elephant's head, he combined traits from several earlier Vedic gods. Another new Hindu god who bore partial animal form—in this case a human body and a monkey's face—was the widely loved and respected Hanuman. Some Vedic writings had mentioned a monkey whom the god Indra had befriended. In classical Hinduism, however, Hanuman emerged as a heroic deity of victory in wartime, the divine model of celibacy, and a champion of righteous causes. The *Hanuman Chalisa*, a sixteenth-century hymn praising him, says in part, "Oh mighty valorous one, of terrific deeds, whose body organs are as strong as diamond. Cure my bad mind oh companion of those with pure mind." Another verse states, "All happiness stay with those who take refuge in you. You are the protector."[9]

Sayana the Myth Teller

One of the foremost Indian writers who compiled versions of some of the many Hindu myths was a widely respected scholar and teacher named Sayana, also sometimes called Sayanacarya. A native of southern India, in the region of modern Bellary, he flourished during the mid-1300s. His works, penned in Sanskrit, caused later scholars to consider him the father of European Vedic scholarship. (Although he never actually visited Europe, his interpretations of the Hindu myths were the ones that most influenced later European thinkers and writers.)

The exact number of texts Sayana produced is unclear, but more than a hundred have been attributed to him over the years. Among them are extensive commentaries on the Vedas, some of which may have been written by his students. His principal work is the *Vedartha Prakasha*, which roughly translates to *What the Vedas Are About*. Throughout this enormous compilation of texts, various gods and their exploits are mentioned—information that introduced new generations of Indians to the old myths. This work is so revered in India and among all Hindus that modern Indian cultural commentator Raghavendra Hebbalalu has called it "the zenith of the exalted achievements" of medieval India.

Raghavendra Hebbalalu, "Madhava-Vidyaranya: Contributions to Culture," *Prekshaa*, August 25, 2016. www.prekshaa.in.

Crucial Spiritual Ideas and Written Texts

Just as some of the Vedic gods carried over into Hinduism, various Vedic spiritual ideas and prominent religious texts did as well. One of the most crucial of those spiritual concepts was reincarnation. The exact way that Vedic worshippers defined it remains somewhat unclear, but Hindus came to view it as the repeated rebirth of a human soul, or *atman*, following death. In other words, when someone dies, his or her soul switches to another physical body, and when that second body expires, the soul moves to a third body, and so forth.

That evolving spirit, which strives to improve itself over time, is largely indestructible. According to the famous Hindu text the Bhagavad Gita, "As a man discards worn-out clothes to put on new and different ones, so the embodied self discards its worn-out bodies to take on other new ones." Weapons cannot cut the *atman*, the passage continues, and fire will not burn it to ashes. Rather, "it is enduring, all-pervasive, immovable, and timeless."[10]

Of the Vedic literary works that transferred to Hinduism, the most important were the Vedas. Their numerous hymns and prayers to the gods also contain various myths associated with those deities. In addition, Vedic priests and thinkers produced other writings that over time contributed to Hindu beliefs and customs. Noteworthy among those are the Upanishads, consisting of scholarly explanations of and commentaries on the Vedas.

Later Literary Works and Worship Customs

Other key Hindu literary works developed later, during the faith's thousand-year-long classical period. By far the most significant of these are two long, colorful epic poems that were composed in Sanskrit and contain a large portion of Hindu mythology and other religious lore. The first of those epics, the Ramayana, was compiled in stages between about the fourth century BCE and the third century CE. It contains almost twenty-four thousand verses.

The other great Hindu epic, the Mahabharata, developed between roughly the fourth century BCE and the fourth century CE. It is the longest epic poem ever created. With more than 1.8 million words, forming over one hundred thousand verses, it is ten times longer than the famous Greek epics, the *Iliad* and the *Odyssey*, combined. The many legends of gods, demons, and human heroes in the Ramayana and the Mahabharata came to shape Hindu thought and practice much as the tales in the Bible shaped Christian beliefs and values.

Along with these new literary texts, as Hinduism matured it developed some new worship customs and artistic styles. The most prominent combination of those two aspects of the faith was the design and construction of temples for worship that began in earnest across India during the 300s CE. These splendid structures gave the fast-emerging faith a public face and more highly developed spiritual identity.

During the Vedic period and early Hindu centuries, families had worshipped either in their homes or at modest altars erected in fields or caves. In contrast, building a large-scale, sturdy, magnificently decorated temple required the talents and labor of the entire community and gave those people a powerful sense of overall communal spirit. "Temples inevitably became the very center of a community," writer Mark Cartwright points out. "Accordingly, their upkeep was guaranteed by land grants and endowments from the ruling class, as indicated by inscriptions on many temples." Furthermore, he states, "The temple was considered the dwelling place of a particular god. It was, therefore, a sacred place where heaven and earth meet and, as a god's home, it must be a suitably splendid palace. The needs of the god would, additionally, be supervised by a dedicated body of priests who attended the temple."[11]

Building towering temples was a way to bring all members of a community together in common purpose. This magnificent example, erected between 950 and 1050 CE, is one of the twenty-five temples in Khajuraho, in north-central India.

Hindu temples also educated worshippers by providing them with vital information about their faith. An analogy would be the stained glass windows in Christian churches. They are not only decorative but also help teach the faithful by depicting scenes from key Bible stories. In the same manner, the sculptured figures on and inside Hindu temples portray the myths of deities like Shiva, Vishnu, Mitra, Ganesha, and Hanuman.

All of these developments mark Hinduism's classical and medieval eras. It was during these eras that Hinduism emerged as a fully developed world religion. "From this period," noted scholar of Hinduism Gavin Flood writes, "we can recognize many elements in present day Hinduism."[12] These include many of the tales that make up Hindu mythology.

CHAPTER TWO

The Creation of the World and Humans

The creation of the world and living things, including humans, is one of the central themes of all world mythologies. Yet the concept of creation differs widely from one religion and mythology to another. In the Abrahamic faiths—Judaism, Christianity, and Islam, all based on descent from the patriarch Abraham—the creation is a single, clear-cut event. "In the beginning God created the heavens and the earth," it states in the Judeo-Christian Old Testament. "And God said, 'Let there be light,' and there was light."[13]

In Hindu mythology, by contrast, there are multiple creations, with separate stories for each. In part, this is because Hinduism initially developed from local religious traditions scattered across India, and each region had somewhat different creation tales. Also, Hinduism views the universe, and time itself, as eternal, with no set beginning or end. In this scenario, the world begins; undergoes decline and destruction; is later reborn in a new beginning, which, in turn, is destroyed and reborn; and so forth. To Hindus, therefore, noted Indian mythologist Devdutt Pattanaik explains,

> beginning refers to the beginning of a phase, not beginning of the world itself. In Abrahamic mythology, the world comes into being from nothingness by the will of God; and

it will end in nothingness. There is a starting and an end point. [In comparison] in Hinduism it is a line, eternal and even repetitive. This difference in the notion of time, explains the difference in the creation myths.[14]

A few of the Hindu creation myths developed during the Vedic era and were directly related to Vedic deities. Perhaps the most prominent creation tale from that period envisioned the existence of a primeval golden egg, which floated in a vast universal sea for a thousand years and then burst open. Out came the first divine being, named Purusha. He soon divided himself in half; the two then proceeded to mate and give rise to other gods as well as to animals and people.

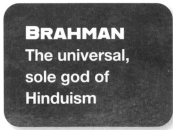

BRAHMAN
The universal, sole god of Hinduism

The Main Hindu Creator Gods

Although this story and other early Vedic creation tales survived into the Hindu classical age, most people came to view them as very old folktales rather than as stories that explained creation. As Hinduism evolved and beliefs and even deities changed, new creation stories also developed. The later accounts were more complex and more mystical than those of Vedic times.

Unlike the early Vedic peoples and other ancient cultures that recognized and worshipped many separate gods, the Hindus believed that only one god created and controlled the universe. They called him Brahman, or the *ishvara* (meaning "universal spirit").

VISHNU
One of Hinduism's three main creator deities, he is often called "the Preserver" or "the Protector"

But their myths include many other deities. These deities are not considered to be separate entities, however. In the Hindu faith, deities such as Ganesha, Shiva, Vishnu, Mitra, and others represent various manifestations, disguises, or

The three deities making up Hinduism's sacred trinity, the Trimurti, are depicted in these ornate Indian figurines fashioned in the early twentieth century. Left to right, they represent Brahma, Shiva, and Vishnu.

avatars of the sole god. That is, Brahman is able to exist on many different levels simultaneously and to play a different role on each level. Moreover, several of those roles, or avatars, have been creator deities.

The most prominent of the Hindu creator gods are the three making up Hinduism's sacred trinity, which is known as the Trimurti. Its three members are Brahma (not to be confused with the overarching sole god, Brahman), Vishnu, and Shiva. Each of these major avatars of the *ishvara* has figured prominently in Hindu creation tales.

Eternity and Endless Cycles

Both Brahma and Vishnu play crucial roles in perhaps the best known of those stories. Because of the Hindu conceptions of time and eternity, the act of creation by Brahma, with Vishnu's aid, is part of a repeating cycle. Hindus believe there have been in the past—and will be again in the future—an infinite number of such

25

Shiva the True Creator?

Most of the Hindu creation stories feature Brahma as the primary creator, but a few myths claim that Vishnu did more creating than Brahma. Shiva's role is almost always that of destroyer in preparation for the next round of creation. However, one Hindu myth, recounted here by modern mythologist Angus Sutherland, claims that Shiva overshadowed his fellow members of the Trimurti when it came to creating things.

> When the world suffered a periodic destruction, Brahma (the Creator amongst the Hindu Trinity) saw Vishnu lying on the coils of infinity, and smiling. He greeted Brahma . . . [and] the two began to argue over which of them is more important, until unexpectedly a gigantic shining column appeared without beginning or end. They decided to examine its limits. That was thought to end the gods' dispute. Vishnu changed into a wild boar and for thousands of years he searched (unsuccessfully) for the base of this column. Brahma, on the other hand, took the form of a white goose, rose high, and for a thousand years he tried in vain to find the upper end of the column. Then, suddenly, Shiva emerged out of the center of the column and declared that only he is the true creator and destroyer of the world. He is a form of himself; he is eternal and exists at different levels of reality. At the end, Brahma was punished for a lie and his pretending to be the greatest.

Angus Sutherland, "Shiva—Hindu God Who Resides in Every Being and in All Things," Ancient Pages, April 8, 2019. ww.ancientpages.com.

cycles. Therefore, the universe comes into being, exists for a set time, and then is destroyed, after which a new universe begins, which itself is destroyed, and so forth. In theory, Brahman (the *ishvara*) exists, untouched, in the background throughout these repeating cycles. But his avatars, including Brahma and Vishnu, are themselves destroyed at the end of a cycle and are reborn at the start of a new one. Shiva prepares for the next cycle by destroying the existing universe after it has run its course.

Each new cycle of creation and existence lasts an untold number of years. No one knows how many, but it is thought to be somewhere in the hundreds of billions, if not more. It is divided into various smaller subcycles. Of these, the most important is called a *kalpa*. As Veronica Ions explains, a *kalpa* is

> one mere day in the life of Brahma [within a given cycle] but is equivalent to 4.32 billion years on earth. When Brahma wakes the three worlds (heavens, middle, and lower regions) are created, and when he sleeps, they are reduced to chaos. All beings who have not obtained liberation [i.e., become one with the *ishvara*] are judged and must prepare for rebirth according to their deserts [what they deserve] when Brahma wakes on the new day.[15]

The Sea, the Snake, and the Lotus

Each time that Brahma awakes on a new day, ready to begin a new creation, all that exists at that moment is darkness. Within that ostensibly unending night lays a vast, dark ocean that has no edges or shores. That boundless sea is composed of a chaotic mixture of the wreckage of the universe that was destroyed by Shiva at the close of the last great cycle. Suddenly, Brahma floats to the surface wrapped in the petals of a large lotus flower. As Brahma climbs from the flower and looks around, he notices a huge snake—a cobra—floating in the sea. As the god approaches, he sees that something is nestled within the serpent's coils. It is Vishnu, who is fast asleep while the snake protects him. Brahma marvels that his fellow avatar looks so peaceful and calm and seemingly undisturbed by dreams or by anything else.

After a while, Brahma notices something else arise from the sea's depths. It is a humming sound—an om—which grows louder and louder over time. When the sound reaches a fever pitch, Vishnu abruptly wakes up; at that instant, the first dawn in the new cycle occurs, ending the gloomy night. Together, Brahma and Vishnu begin to create a new world and the beings to populate it.

In a popular variant of the story, the snake and sleeping Vishnu appear first. After the god awakes, he sees a lotus flower rising from his navel. Inside the flower is Brahma, who also awakes and greets Vishnu. The latter tells Brahma that it is now time to begin a new cycle of creation. Brahma agrees and proceeds to split the lotus into three sections, of which one becomes the earth's surface, the second part forms the sky, and the third fragment grows into the heavens above the sky.

In one of Hinduism's creation stories, Vishnu appears first and sees a lotus flower rising from his navel. Inside that flower rests Brahma. This Indian painting shows Brahma's many-sided personality inside the lotus.

Whichever version of the story is told, the creation always takes place in India, which Hindus believe lies at the midpoint of both earth and the universe. "In the center of the world is Mount Meru," Ions continues,

> whose summit, 84,000 leagues high, is the site of Brahma's heaven, which is encircled by the River Ganges and surrounded by the cities of Indra and [the cities of] other deities. The foothills of Mount Meru are the home of benevolent spirits, such as Gandharvas, while the valleys are peopled by the demons. The whole world is supported by the hood of the great serpent Shesha.[16]

In still other versions of the creation, the serpent is coiled on the back of a huge tortoise. Or the whole system is supported by four monstrous elephants. Or it is supported by four giant humanoid creatures who cause earthquakes when they move.

Ignorance, Night, and the Forces of Evil

In the main Hindu creation stories, thanks to Brahma, the barren earth rapidly fills with living things. He covers the plains with grass, fills the meadows with flowers, and fashions vast forests containing millions of trees. Then he makes animals, including cattle, sheep, elephants, and other mammals; birds; insects; and sea creatures.

Hindu mythology contains an important variation of this creation story. In it, Brahma is forced to carry out some extra acts of creation not long after the initial main one. This is because he makes some unfortunate mistakes in his first try. His principal error is to have a moment of distraction in which he is not concentrating on the work at hand. In one myth, this mistake causes a negative being or force—Ignorance—to emerge. Brahma regrets this

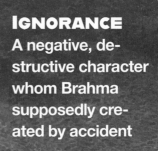

IGNORANCE
A negative, destructive character whom Brahma supposedly created by accident

Alternate Mythical First Humans

Although Manu is cited as the first human in most Hindu creation myths, a few alternate creation stories have survived in which other individuals claim that honor. The most common one is Yama, said to be the son of the sun god Surya. According to Yama's story, which dates from the Vedic age, he married his sister, Yami, and their offspring began to populate the world. Many modern experts think that the core of Yama's tale was not Indian in origin but likely came from Persia (Iran). An almost identical Persian myth names Yima and Yimeh as the first man and woman, and it is possible that Persian merchants or other travelers brought that tale to India during the Vedic period.

A later Hindu myth builds on Yama's initial story, claiming that he was not necessarily the first man, but he *was* the first human to die. After passing on, he then became the lord of the dead, a minor deity. At first, he was pictured as decent and just. But over time his character hardened and became fearsome, mean-spirited, and at times even frightening. Hindu artists came to show Yama with four arms, large fangs, a huge frown, and carrying weapons, most often a club or sword.

and seeks to remedy the situation by destroying that unwanted creature. Somehow, however, Ignorance manages to survive and evolves into Night, which gives rise to and shelters sinister and evil forces that lurk there ever after. These nefarious forces want to kill Brahma, and they make several attempts on his life. To counter them, therefore, he begins creating again, and this time he fashions various divine and angel-like beings, which thereafter keep the evil ones in check.

In a popular variant of this tale, Mark Cartwright points out, Ignorance does not appear. Instead, the demons and other dark forces "were born from Brahma's thigh and so he abandoned his own body which then became Night. After Brahma created good gods he abandoned his body once again, which then became Day, hence demons gain the ascendancy at night and gods, the forces of goodness, rule the day."[17]

Manu and the Emergence of Humans

By the time Brahma and Vishnu had made the earth, mountains, forests, flowers, and animals, creation was almost complete. What was missing was a race of humans to enjoy the wonders of nature and to worship the gods. Thus, Brahma created the first human—a man named Manu.

A charming Hindu myth that closely parallels a well-known Christian Bible story explains how Manu eventually set in motion the emergence of the human race. One day Manu was out for a walk on the bank of a river when he heard a small voice begging him for help. Looking around, the man saw a tiny fish staring up at him from the water's edge. The fish asked Manu to keep him as a pet. That way, it would not be eaten by bigger fish and, as a result, would almost surely live longer. Manu agreed and made a home for the fish in a basin of water in his hut.

One of the more popular Hindu myths tells how the first human, Manu, found a fish and saved its life. That fish was really the god Vishnu in disguise, as illustrated in this painting showing the blue-skinned deity with a fish's lower body.

To thank the man for saving him, the fish told him a secret of nature known only to animals. A huge flood would occur soon that would cover the earth's entire surface. Manu should build a boat, the fish warned, which would allow him to survive. The man did as the fish suggested and, just as Noah did in the Bible, constructed a sturdy boat; sure enough, the great flood came. Thanks to the fish, Manu survived. As the water subsided, the fish suddenly transformed into a magnificent, glowing being. "I am Vishnu, the Preserver," he told Manu (in an excerpt from the Bhagavad Gita). "I appeared to you in the shape of a fish to protect you from the deluge. You are destined to start new races to inhabit the world."[18]

MANU
In a number of Hindu creation myths, the first human created by Brahma

Vishnu's prediction came to pass. When the waters completely subsided, Brahma made a young woman named Shatarupa. She became Manu's wife, and together they produced children who, in their turn, had more offspring. In that way, the human race began. The grand process of creation set in motion by the primary avatars of the sole god—the mystical *ishvara*—was at last complete.

CHAPTER THREE

Tales of Love and Lovers

"Perhaps no other faith glorifies the idea of love between the sexes as Hinduism," remarks Indian writer Subhamoy Das, an expert on the history of that religion. "This is evident from the amazing variety of mythical love stories that abound in Sanskrit literature, which is undoubtedly one of the richest treasure hoards of exciting love tales."[19] Indeed, many of the large-scale ancient Hindu texts, especially the enormous Ramayana, contain love stories. Some of those relationships are between two gods, others involve human lovers, and still others deal with deities who fall in love with mortals.

A number of these amorous tales feature the Hindu god of love and desire, Kama, a son of the deities Vishnu and Lakshmi. Kama frequently arouses romantic feelings in others—both divine and human. In Hindu art, he is most often pictured as a handsome youth with red or green skin, and he is armed with a bow made of sugarcane and arrowheads made of flowers.

Even when Kama does not physically appear in a myth, it is understood that he likely had something to do with bringing the lovers together. Sometimes those characters find happy endings, and other times they suffer Romeo-and-Juliet-type tragedies. Thus, the diverse ways that love is depicted in the myths mirrors

Kama, the Hindu god of love and desire, was said to be the son of the deities Vishnu and Lakshmi. This eighteenth-century drawing of Kama shows him riding a parrot, an animal Hindus associate with sexual desire.

the complexity and fickle qualities of love in real life. As Indian columnist and myth teller Kavita Kane puts it,

> Such tales of love, and love lost, are numerous and scattered throughout [Hindu mythology], where in each case love is displayed in all its splendor and shades. Love [in those tales] is important and nourishing, sometimes even hurtful, deadly, and destructive. However, love [is] vital to the scheme of existence, and the smallest love story in the [Hindu] epics . . . is a homage [tribute] to [that deep human] emotion.[20]

Blinded by Her Husband

Nowhere in Indian lore are the complexities and uncertainties of love depicted more vividly than in the story of Surya and Sanjana. The latter was the lovely daughter of Vishvakarman, the deity of creative power and the god who was said to have taught early humans how to erect large-scale buildings and monuments. Vishvakarman desired that his daughter marry a fellow divinity, so he arranged for her to wed the sun god Surya.

SANJANA
The wife of the sun god Surya; she was unable to look directly at her husband's blindingly bright image

Once she got to know her husband, Sanjana felt genuine love for him. However, because his visage was so overpoweringly bright, she had to look away, or seriously squint, when he came near. That irritated Surya, but he came to accept it. The couple

Yama Kumar and the Princess

One of the most popular love stories from Hindu mythology tells about how Yama, deity of death, married a mortal woman. They had a son named Yama Kumar, who grew up to be a physician and an expert on medicinal herbs. One day the young man heard that a princess in a neighboring kingdom had become extremely ill and that her doctors were unable to heal her. The good-hearted Yama Kumar journeyed to that land and offered to try to cure the young woman; her grateful father, the king, gave him a free hand. But as Yama Kumar approached the princess's bed, he was shocked to see his own father—the death god—standing in the room, ready to take her to the underworld. The young man pleaded with Yama to spare the princess. Because he loved his son, the god agreed to let her live for three more days. After that, Yama Kumar refused to leave the princess's bedside and tried every medicine he could think of—but none worked. At the close of the third day, he saw his father, Yama, approaching to snatch away her soul. Thinking quickly, the young man tricked the god of death into believing that someone he detested was in the room. Yama wanted to avoid seeing that person, so he hurried away; when he did so, the princess's condition rapidly improved. After a few weeks she regained her health. She later married Yama Kumar, and they enjoyed long, happy lives together.

had a son they named Manu. Later, Sanjana became pregnant a second time and gave birth to twins, a boy and a girl.

Unfortunately for Sanjana, her husband's intense light and heat eventually bothered her so much that she closed her eyes and kept her distance when he entered the room. That angered Surya, and he loudly scolded his wife. This reaction, coupled with the fact that she could never look directly at him, made her very

Sanjara's husband, the sun-god Surya, is frequently depicted in Hindu art. This modern painting, like most before it, shows him holding lotus flowers and seated in his seven-horse chariot. His faithful driver, Aruna, steers the vehicle.

unhappy; she decided she had to remedy the situation. As modern Indian myth teller Shreekant Vijaykar writes,

> She could take it no more. The constant glare darkened her and sapped her energy. She was now called Sandhya, (evening) due to her hue. Yet, she did not wish to leave, for she did not want to offend her husband. Finally, after some deliberation, she came up with a solution. From her body, she created an image, a clone of herself, just a bit darker, and called her Chhaya (shadow).[21]

Fooled by the Ruse

Chhaya now took Sanjana's place in the house and pretended to be her. Meanwhile, the real Sanjana snuck away and journeyed deep into a nearby forest. There, she turned herself into a well-proportioned horse, hoping that the disguise would keep her husband from finding her.

This worry turned out to be misplaced because Surya was completely fooled by the ruse. Assuming that Chhaya was his real wife, he went about his daily activities, which included making love to Chhaya. Hence, she bore him three children. However, she then made the mistake of treating her own offspring well but neglecting Sanjana's three children. As a result, Manu and his siblings began to suspect that Chhaya was not their real mother, and they imparted their doubts about her to their father.

Surya, who trusted his children's instincts, confronted Chhaya and demanded that she tell him the truth. Terrified of his divine wrath, the fake wife admitted she was not the real Sanjana and told Surya the whole story of the deception. This made the sun god extremely unhappy because he did truly love the real Sanjana.

Surya decided that he must find his wife and searched all the nearby villages. He also checked with his father-in-law, Vishvakarman, and confirmed she had not fled to her parents' home. Next, Surya entered the forest in search of his lost love. After a while he learned that she had transformed herself into a horse, and he proceeded to take a horse's form himself. In so doing, he greatly reduced his glare, which was no longer blinding to behold.

Not long afterward, the husband and wife, both still in the guise of horses, encountered each other in a quiet glade. Surya was happy to find the woman he loved, and Sanjana was overjoyed that she could comfortably look directly at her husband. They decided to live there in the forest, in horse form, for a few more years. Then they assumed their normal forms and returned home, where they lived happily with their children. (Chhaya was allowed to stay on as Surya's second wife.)

Heer and Ranjha's Forbidden Love

Although Surya and Sanjana's tale had a happy ending, the same cannot be said for another immortal Indian myth—the tragedy of the lovers Heer and Ranjha. The latter was the youngest of eight brothers and his father's favorite son. A carefree youth, Ranjha spent most of this time engaging in his favorite activity—playing his flute.

Ranjha's life changed a great deal when his father passed away, leaving the eight sons to divide up the family's lands. Because his brothers saw him as a worthless dreamer, they gave him the smallest, least productive plot. Frustrated, the young man left his family behind and struck out on his own.

HEER
A young woman who fell in love with a flute player named Ranjha and met a tragic end

After a long journey, Ranjha came to a town called Jhang. There, he met a well-to-do farmer named Sayyal, who was looking for someone to manage his stables. Needing work, Ranjha took the job. A few days later he met Sayyal's stunningly beautiful daughter, Heer, and the two young people swiftly fell deeply in love. Heer worried that her father would disapprove of her being with a mere stable boy, so the lovers agreed to keep their relationship secret.

The Genius of the Punjab

The tragic love story of Heer and Ranjha is one of the most famous and cherished myths of India and Pakistan. Various versions of it were told over the centuries, but by far the most popular was the one by Punjabi poet Waris Shah (1722–1798). (Punjabi, spoken today by approximately 125 million people, is the most common language used in Pakistan, which used to be part of India. Both modern Indians and Pakistanis revere Shah and his works.)

Shah was born in a small town in the Punjab, then part of India and today mostly in Pakistan. After receiving an education, he moved to the Punjabi town of Malka Hans, where he dwelled in a small room near the local mosque until his death. It was there that he composed his now immortal version of *Heer and Ranjha*, told in verse. Later translated into many languages, it became one of the most popular love stories in the world. As one modern Pakistani commentator puts it, "What Waris Shah wrote 250 years ago in a small village has stood the test of time. Rather it has proved to be the best creative expression of Punjabi genius."

Quoted in Furquan Ameen Siddiqui, "A Punjabi Saga of Timeless, Tragic Love: 250 Years of Waris Shah's Heer," *Hindustan Times*, August 20, 2016. www.hindustantimes.com.

This arrangement worked for more than a year. But then one day Heer's uncle, Kaido, saw the couple embracing in the stable and immediately told her parents what he had seen. Sayyal told his daughter that she must stop seeing Ranjha because he was not good enough for either her or the family. But she refused to stop seeing the man she loved. Her parents then took her to the town's official who oversaw the local social laws. Heer told the official the same thing she had told her parents—that she loved Ranjha and wanted to remain with him.

The parents now took matters into their own hands and arranged for Heer to marry a respectable local landowner named Saida, a man Heer had never even met. On the day of the marriage ceremony, she complained to the town's officials. She told them that she could not marry Saida because she was already wed to Ranjha, a marriage she was convinced was approved by

God himself. Both the officials and Heer's parents ignored her pleas, went through with the ceremony, and allowed Saida to take her to his home.

The Basket of Candy

Hearing about what had transpired, Ranjha was naturally both angry and heartbroken. He went running into a nearby forest, where he considered taking his own life. But soon he encountered a group of Hindu monks, and when they asked him to join their number, he agreed. Ranjha pierced his ears and covered his body in fine ash, customs followed by the monks. He also followed their lead and traveled from one town to another, begging for food.

As fate would have it, many months later Ranjha arrived at Saida's house to beg, not realizing it was where Heer was living. The housekeeper instantly recognized him. She did not agree with the cruel way Heer had been forced into marriage and dragged away to a strange man's house. The housekeeper helped Heer and Ranjha to reunite, and the lovers escaped into the forest.

It did not take long for the local authorities to find the young couple. They brought Heer and Ranjha to the kingdom's ruler for judgment. To the surprise of all involved, he agreed with the lovers' argument that they had long been wed in God's eyes. He therefore freed them and pronounced the marriage between Heer and Saida null and void.

Heer and Ranjha soon had their own marriage ceremony, and all would have ended well had it not been for Heer's parents. They felt that dissolving the first marriage and allowing Heer to marry her lover had ruined their reputation. To save face, the parents sent the newlyweds a basket of candy that had been laced with a deadly poison. When Heer ate some of the candy, she fell dead beside her husband. Realizing what had happened, he purposely ate some of the candy too and died holding his wife's body.

Wrongs That Needed to Be Righted

The terrible crime perpetrated by Heer's parents remained a potent reminder in both Hindu and world mythology that evil always lurks in the shadows, ready to try to destroy the forces of good and love. At the same time, no character in world mythology worked more relentlessly to eradicate evil and live for love than the Hindu deity Vishnu. This was especially true when he assumed the form of Krishna, the eighth of his many incarnations, or earthly disguises.

KRISHNA
The eighth incarnation of the god Vishnu

As Krishna, from the very start the god found himself at the heart of appalling wrongs that he felt needed to be righted. For example, Kamsa, the wicked ruler of the Indian kingdom of Mathura, heard a prophecy early in his reign that predicted he would die at the hands of the eighth child of his own sister, Devaki. The king therefore became determined to slay the child right after it was born.

This plan did not come to fruition, however, because Devaki's eighth infant was none other than Krishna. As soon as he was born, his mother switched him with the newborn child of a cowherd and his wife who lived in the nearby region of Gokul. That couple raised Krishna, whom they did not realize was divine, as their own son. Meanwhile, King Kamsa thought he had killed his sister's eighth child; nevertheless, to be sure there was no margin for error, he ordered all the male babies in the kingdom to be murdered.

A few years after committing that evil act, Kamsa received word that the child might still be alive, although the boy's location remained a mystery. The king thus prayed to a horde of demons to come to his aid. These hideous creatures tracked Krishna down and attacked him. But he easily destroyed them, one after another.

Krishna and the Cowgirls

Meanwhile, Krishna grew up as a cowherd in Gokul in the midst of a society dominated by young women. The evil king's murder of the male babies had left behind mostly female children, so the boy was the only young male in his town. Coupled with his incredible good looks, that made him extremely popular among the local *gopis*, or female cowherds, who milked the cows and made the butter. All were from poor families having no social standing. But that did not matter to Krishna, for he viewed all humans, no matter their background, as equal in worth.

Practically every cowgirl dreamed of becoming the boy's girl-friend and later his wife. Therefore, they all tended to put up with the many playful pranks Krishna pulled on them. In one

The cowgirl Radha stands beside the fun-loving Krishna, whose blue skin identifies him as an incarnation of Vishnu. In one popular tale, Krishna swiftly grew extra arms so he could dance with many cowgirls at the same time.

of the best-known pranks, he swiped their clothes while they were swimming in the local river. In order to retrieve their garments, each had to walk naked from the water to where Krishna was holding the clothes, which gave him the eyeful that he had wanted.

Krishna also attended dances with the cowgirls. At first, he did not want to seem to play favorites. So, as a dance progressed, he instantly sprouted dozens of extra arms, so that he was able to hold and dance with all of the girls at the same time. Eventually, however, he fell in love with one particular cowgirl, Radha. Although the other girls were disappointed that he had not chosen any of them, they wished the young couple well and, when possible, walked with and guarded them. As described by Shahrukh Husain, one day Krishna took Radha in his arms "and embraced her tenderly while all the other girls gazed longingly at the two of them from behind the trees and bushes of the forest. Krishna knew that they were there and to please them, he created many images of himself so that each girl thought that she held his hand."[22]

RADHA
The cowgirl from Gokul with whom Krishna fell in love

Later, Krishna made it possible for Radha's soul to leave her mortal body. It flew to him and merged with his own divine being. He exclaimed that thereafter, despite her coming from a poor family, they would never be separated. In this way, Vishnu, disguised as Krishna, demonstrated that true love and devotion were ultimately more important in life than high birth and wealth.

CHAPTER FOUR

Stalwart Heroes Versus Foul Demons

Heroes who fight on the side of goodness and right abound in the huge corpus of Hindu myths. These courageous characters are needed because of the existence of evil creatures and forces in those stories. Among them are the *asuras*, the divine beings who started out as benevolent gods but later turned on and opposed the good deities.

Much worse, however, is a race of foul demons called *rakshasas*. One major explanation for their existence is that their creation was an accident. Brahma, the famous creator god, fell asleep, the story goes, and his moist, heavy breath gave rise to those hideous beings. To the horror and regret of their victims, the *rakshasas* were extremely strong, sported sharp fangs and claws, had wings, and liked the taste of human flesh. They also wielded potent magic that allowed them to change their shape and, therefore, made them very hard to capture or kill.

The great Hindu epic the Ramayana tells how the demons created their own kingdom on an island fortress called Lanka. Their king—the ugliest and most vicious of their number—was the fearsome Ravana. He desired to attack the human kingdoms and

RAVANA
The king of the demons and lord of the dark kingdom of Lanka

turn their populations into slaves and a food source. But several stalwart, morally upright warriors, some divine and others mortal, were determined to keep that awful outcome from coming to pass. Following in the footsteps of the god Indra, who had slain the repulsive monster Vritra, they fought back against the demons in a series of momentous, bloody battles.

Bhima Battles Baka

Among the greatest of those demon-fighting warriors was Bhima, a member of the Pandavas, a widely respected ancient Indian family line of community leaders and warriors. Word reached him one day that a demon named Baka had entered the section of India where the Pandavas dwelled. Most people, including Bhima, had heard stories about Baka, who—prior to this—had confined his murderous activities to the plateau region of southern India. Reports claimed that the creature towered more than 20 feet (6 m) tall and had red stains on his lips and chin from the blood that dripped when he was devouring human flesh and organs.

A nineteenth-century Indian water color depicts the bloody battle of Lanka, in which the heroic Rama, seen at left with the bow, and his followers defeat an opposing army of demons, led by the repulsive Ravana, riding the chariot.

Recently, Baka had suddenly appeared in a village not far from Bhima's home and demanded that the local elders make a deal with him. If they wanted to escape complete destruction, they must provide him with the food he required to satisfy his appetite. The daily menu, he told them, consisted of two wagons filled with assorted vegetables, plus one human. Feeling like they had no other choice, the elders agreed to the demon's demands. Already, more than two dozen villagers had met a gruesome end in the monster's stomach, and Bhima decided he must intervene before any other innocent people died.

Hurrying to the afflicted village, the muscular but agile young man met with the elders and convinced them to send *him* as Ba-

Key Hindu Villains: The Demons

The frightening and lethal demons called *rakshasas* make up one of the darkest forces in Hindu mythology. Hairy and otherwise gorilla-like in appearance, they supposedly once caused all sorts of misery among humans before heroes like Bhima and Rama fought and killed them. Noted modern myth teller Veronica Ions further describes these key Hindu villains:

> They often adopt disguises to hide their monstrosity—especially their womenfolk, who sometimes succeed in undermining the defenses of mortal men by bewitching them. . . . Without disguises, however, they present a great variety of deformity. Some are dwarfs, others like beanstalks; some fat, others emaciated; some have over-long arms; some only one eye, or only one ear; some have monstrous bellies; some have crooked legs, some one leg, some three and four; some have serpents' heads, others have donkeys', horses', or elephants' heads. Just as their appearance varies, so do their functions. There are the [*darbas*], who haunt cemeteries and eat the bodies of the dead. There are the *panis,* aerial [flying] demons who inspire foolish actions and encourage slander and disbelief. . . . There are the *grahas,* evil spirits who often cluster about the god of war, Karttikeya, and who possess people's souls and make them insane.

Veronica Ions, *Indian Mythology*. New York: Peter Bedrick, 1984, p. 116.

ka's next victim. The next morning Bhima removed his fine satin robes and dressed like a simple villager. Then he waited with the vegetable-laden wagons in the place in the forest where the demon regularly collected the food.

After a few minutes, Bhima felt the ground vibrating and suspected that the minor earth tremor was caused by the pounding of Baka's enormous legs and feet on the ground as he approached. Sure enough, the demon emerged from a stand of trees, his gaping mouth already dripping saliva in anticipation of his morning meal. As he moved toward Bhima, the latter told him to leave the region at once; if Baka stayed, the young man warned, it would be a fatal mistake. The demon's eyes widened, and he stopped short. Clearly, he was surprised to hear a human threaten him that way, and his hideous face displayed a broad scowl.

Baka now emitted a low-throated growl and rushed at Bhima, intending to kill him with one blow and then eat him. But the giant had met his match. As told by Alliance University scholar Karanam Nagaraja Rao, "The duel was fearful. They fought with trees and rocks, and fists of fury. Each tried to crush the other to the dust but each rose up to fight to the finish. Slowly the power of the demon began to wane, and Bhima caught hold of him by his neck and broke his spine to pieces. Baka fell dead on the same field where he had heaped [many] human skulls."[23]

Learning of Bhima's success, the villagers were delighted and heaped praises on him. Not only had the young man eradicated the evil being who had menaced them, but there was also an additional benefit for the residents of the entire region. After Bhima instantly gained a reputation as a demon slayer of the first order, several of Baka's fellow demons fled to some distant caves in the mountains. Fearful that Bhima might hunt them down, they gave up eating people and became vegetarians.

Krishna Versus Keshi

Bhima was only one of several Hindu heroes who became renowned for slaying demons. Of the valiant members of that select group, Krishna, Vishnu's eighth avatar, was one of the more celebrated. When the evil King Kamsa, who had slain all the young boys in his kingdom, found out that Krishna was alive, that ruler asked several demons to track down and kill Krishna. One of those repulsive creatures was Keshi, who looked like a huge, badly misshapen horse with large, sharp teeth.

That horse-monster scoured northern India until he found young Krishna in Gokul. Seeing the boy playing with some cowgirls in a field, Keshi let out a loud screech that frightened the girls away. Krishna, who was totally unafraid of anything, stood his ground and

A key moment in Hindu mythology is captured in this priceless fifth-century sculpture. It shows the heroic Krishna battling the hideous horse-monster Keshi. Krishna inserts his arm, which will rapidly expand, choking the creature.

watched as the hideous-looking horse galloped toward him. At first, Keshi attempted to trample the young man. But this proved fruitless, for Krishna simply sidestepped the beast. Grabbing one of the demon's four legs, the boy swung the creature in the air and tossed him halfway across the field. Keshi landed with a thud and then, angry over that humiliation, attacked again. Several times in a row, Krishna threw the horse-monster to the ground, and each time Keshi grew more incensed and eager to punish and kill the young man.

> **KESHI**
> The horse-shaped demon that Vishnu's avatar Krishna was said to have slain

Finally, the demon decided to use a different strategy. He opened his enormous mouth as wide as possible and ran at Krishna, intending to swallow him whole. But the young man could see what was happening and reacted swiftly. Thrusting one of his arms forward, he jammed it right into the attacker's mouth; less than a second later, Krishna expanded that limb so that it filled Keshi's throat, cutting off his air supply. The horse demon thrashed wildly, desperate for its next breath, which never came. His lifeless body soon collapsed into the dirt, and Krishna withdrew his arm. Having barely worked up a sweat, Vishnu's avatar smiled and returned to playing with the cowgirls. It was not the first evil being he had slain—and it would not be the last.

The Attack of the Demon Army

Every time that a demon like Keshi was eliminated by a hero, the many demons who lived in the dismal land of Lanka became infuriated and talked about achieving revenge. The valiant opponent they most despised and wanted to kill was another of Vishnu's incarnations—Rama. In fact, Rama was India's most renowned demon slayer and, as Mark Cartwright puts it, "the most virtuous hero from Hindu mythology." Along with his wife, Sita, Rama was "a picture of purity and marital devotion."[24]

In fact, Rama was so appealing as a potential husband that even a few female demons were tempted to approach him. This was indeed the case with Surpanakha, sister of Lanka's evil demon ruler, Ravana. One day Rama and his half brother, Lakshmana, were out hunting in the countryside when Surpanakha approached them. She had gone to great pains to use makeup to try to hide her leathery skin, tusks, and cross-eyes and to look as much like a female human as possible. Rama and Lakshmana saw right through her disguise and demanded to know what she wanted. She explained that she had fallen madly in love with Rama and wanted to marry him.

Rama replied that he was already happily married to Sita and was not in need of a second wife (although by custom at that time Indian men *could* have multiple wives). Hearing this, Surpanakha became enraged and began to make threats against Sita. Of the two men, Lakshmana was the first to react. He drew his razor-sharp swords and swiftly sliced off Surpanakha's nose and ears.

The mutilated Surpanakha ran away screaming and hurried back to Lanka, where she told her brother, Ravana, what had happened. He quickly organized an army of more than two thousand demons and ordered them to kill Rama, Lakshmana, Sita, and any other humans who got in their way. Hearing of the horrible horde's approach, Rama donned his golden armor. A passage in the Ramayana describes how he "went out to meet the host, which looked like a mass of dark clouds at sunrise." The demons shot arrows at him but he deflected them with a magical shield. Then, employing an equally magical bow, "he sent forth not one but a hundred arrows at once that flew like serpents through the air, each seeking out its foe and piercing its heart. The demons shrieked and fell, like dry wood consumed by fire. Again and again Rama bent his bow like a sickle, sending forth the deadly arrows that seemed to darken the sun."[25]

Sita's Abduction

Hundreds of demons fell to Rama's arrows, and the rest of the terrified creatures ran for their lives. When they returned to Lanka and told Ravana and Surpanakha what had occurred, the despicable brother and sister became angrier than ever. It was time, Ravana chortled, for him to take matters into his own hands. There was no way, the demon king bragged, that Rama could defeat *him*. After all, Ravana stood several hundred feet tall, had ten heads, twenty arms, and a gigantic mouth containing many sharp teeth. Moreover, Ravana told his sister, he was so strong that he could break off the tops of mountains and hurl them miles away. In addition, Ravana had fought with gods before, including the storm god Indra. None of them had managed

Valmiki the Myth Teller

Valmiki is revered in India and Pakistan in large part because that legendary teacher, sage, and poet is credited with writing the finest and most complete version of the great Sanskrit epic, the Ramayana. The exact century in which Valmiki lived and produced that seminal work remains a matter of debate. Some scholars think he was born during the fifth century BCE; others favor later dates, including as late as the first century BCE. What seems fairly certain is that he did compose the work, based on an attribution to himself in the text.

The most popular of several existing versions of Valmiki's life is a legend in which he began as a poor hunter who made extra money by robbing travelers. One day a band of wise and holy men appeared on the road, and Valmiki prepared to rob them. He was unable to go through with it, however, because an inner voice told him it was wrong. Also, the holy men convinced him that he must end up paying a steep price for committing sins such as robbery. Now reformed, over time Valmiki became a sage and holy man himself and compiled the large body of popular myths that became the immortal Ramayana.

to kill the demon king, Ravana boasted, and it would be no different with Rama. In fact, this time it would be Rama who would die, Ravana predicted.

First, Ravana reasoned, he must draw Rama out and at the same time throw him off balance by filling his mind with worry about his wife's safety. To that end, the demon king disguised himself as a Hindu monk and traveled to northern India. There, he came upon Sita in the forest where she took her daily walks. Be-

In this exciting scene from the immortal Ramayana, the valiant Rama and his faithful companion Hanuman oppose the horrible demon Ravana, who had kidnapped Sita. The demon could not resist the mighty Rama and was defeated.

lieving he could take on a charming personality and lure her away from her husband, he freely admitted his true identity. According to the Ramayana, after introducing himself, he told her,

> Beyond the sea, on the summit of a mountain, stands my splendid city, Lanka, filled with every delight. O beautiful one, come and live with me there as my chief queen and forget the lot of mortal women. Think no more of Rama, [whose] end is near. I, the lord of all demons, have come to you, pierced by the shafts of love; therefore yield to me, fair princess![26]

Not surprisingly, Ravana's supposedly pretty speech did not impress Sita in the least. She rejected his offer for her to visit Lanka, so he promptly kidnapped her and took her there by force. Hearing about her abduction, Rama and Lakshmana wasted no time in raising an army with which to invade Ravana's kingdom. Among the troops was a contingent of monkeys, led by their general, Hanuman. Because he was a son of the wind god Vayu, Hanuman was able to fly, so Rama sent him ahead to inform Sita that she would soon be liberated. A few hours later, Hanuman quietly entered Ravana's palace, making sure to avoid the demon guards. Rama was on his way with a huge army, he told Sita, so she should take heart.

Ravana's Downfall

The next day, Rama and his forces assaulted Lanka. In response, Ravana unleashed his thousands of demon soldiers. As the bloody battle raged, Ravana's repulsive son, Indrajit, searched for Rama and Lakshmana, hoping to kill them. Although he failed to do so, he did badly wound them both. Seeing this, Hanuman flew at top speed to the summit of a nearby mountain where there grew a magical herb that only the gods and their kin knew existed. Rushing back to the battle, the monkey general applied the herb to Rama's and Lakshmana's wounds, and they instantly healed.

Within a few hours, a majority of the strongest demons lay dead, and it was clear that Rama's forces were winning the conflict. Consumed with rage, Ravana berated the remaining demons, calling them worthless slugs. He shouted that the only way to eliminate Rama and his followers was to do it himself. Stepping out into an open section of the field, he challenged Rama to single combat, and Rama readily obliged. According to the Ramayana,

> There followed a struggle as had never been seen on earth, when those two warriors tried to kill each other. Both were skilled archers, both knew all the science of warfare, both had weapons made by the high gods, and neither had ever known defeat. Each sent forth a cloud of arrows as they circled about each other, each had impenetrable armor and stood unwounded.[27]

Eventually, however, Rama's superior strength, combined with the innate power of goodness that pulsed through his body, took a toll on Ravana. As the demon king grew ever more tired, he began to lose his balance and make mistakes. Then Rama let loose a mighty burst of arrows that made the creature fear for his safety for the first time in his long life. Dropping his bow, Ravana fell off his chariot. Rama sped by on his own chariot and lopped off one of the demon's hideous heads. "Finally," in Cartwright's words, "another of Rama's arrows [made] a direct hit on Ravana's chest. The arrow went straight through the demon, travelled over the seas and came straight back into Rama's quiver. Ravana was dead and the world rid of a terrible lawless force."[28] After that, the kingdom of the demons declined and, in due course, dissolved. Although a few demons managed to survive, and still exist today, Rama and the other great ancient heroes had eradicated the worst of their number.

CHAPTER FIVE

The Hindu Myths in Modern Culture

Today Hindu mythology remains as vital and relevant in Indian society as it was in past centuries. This is because those ancient stories are an integral part of both the Hindu faith and Indian culture. "Mythology is the stories, symbols, and rituals that are transmitted over generations by a tribe or a community," says India's leading modern mythologist, Devdutt Pattanaik. "Previously, you thought of them as belonging only to some ancient times, but now I realize that they are a necessary part of human conditions." He adds, "It is through these stories that we give ourselves meaning."[29]

An Unending List of Mythological Fiction

The profound influences of the many Hindu myths on modern culture can conveniently be divided into two broad categories. One consists of those that affect mainly modern Indian culture and nearby southeastern Asian societies that have substantial Hindu populations. The other involves the influences that have affected the larger global culture, including Western (European-based) civilization.

Regarding the first category, the traditional Hindu myths remain well-known throughout most of southern Asia. In India, as well as Pakistan and the island nation of Sri Lanka, for instance,

In one of the many modern retellings of the ancient Hindu myths, members of the popular Shri Ram dance company reenact a scene from the Ramayana in the city of Delhi. Such shows still play to packed houses all across India.

these tales are regularly retold and celebrated in novels, poems, music and dance, movies, television shows, paintings, sculptures, comic books, puppet shows, and other forms of art and media. Sometimes the newer retellings conform to the details of the older versions; other times they contain changes that make them fit better into modern settings. According to Indian-born University of San Francisco scholar Vamsee Juluri,

> Today, as we see publishers with long, seemingly unending lists of mythological fiction and popular TV shows and movies revolving around characters from our epics [including the Ramayana], we find that while our original source might be the same as the one used by those in the past, both our approach to it and the way we consume this genre has changed, with characteristics unique to our times.[30]

Whether presented in traditional or nontraditional settings, the myths have achieved a level of popularity in India that is unheard-of in Western nations. This popularity is especially evident in the country's movies and television shows. In the United States and most of Europe, films with mythological themes are made somewhat infrequently. In comparison, beginning in the early twentieth century and lasting for at least seven decades, well more than half of the films made in India were based on Hindu myths.

Moreover, starting in the 1990s, a new wave of myth-based television shows and movies swept through India and several other southern Asian lands. A large proportion of them were animated. Meanwhile, starting in the early 1980s and continuing to the present, the Amar Chitra Katha graphic novel series, produced in India, has colorfully retold over a thousand traditional myths within the pages of more than 450 separate books. The company has sold in excess of 90 million books in roughly four decades, mainly in southern Asia (although Hindus who live in other parts of the world read them too). This truly extraordinary publishing effort has introduced the Hindu gods and their exploits to several new generations of young readers.

Lively Scenes from the Ramayana

By far the most popular and best-selling stories told in these graphic novels have been those from the two Indian national epics—the Ramayana and the Mahabharata. The same holds true for the numerous modern films, television shows, paintings, traditional novels, and other artistic genres that have tackled the Hindu legends and myths. For example, sculpted scenes from the Ramayana grace all the Hindu temples built during the last two centuries, not only in India but around the globe. That includes the one that opened in Robbinsville, New Jersey, in 2014. Covering some 12,000 square feet (1,114 sq. m), it is the largest Hindu temple in the world.

Lively scenes from the Ramayana have also been depicted in other modern-day artistic venues and media. These have included

Record-Breaking Audiences for Ancient Myths

Ramanand Sagar's Ramayan, which began airing on Indian television in 1987, was one of the most-watched television shows of all time. It was a massive and lavishly produced dramatic film version of the ancient Ramayana. The viewership of 82 percent of India's population was unprecedented and broke all records for the size of television audiences in that nation. Sagar had originally planned to tell the epic's huge story in fifty-two episodes running forty-five minutes each. But the initial episodes were so popular that he and Indian television executives decided to extend the series to seventy-eight episodes. Another pleasant surprise for the filmmakers was that the show was enormously popular outside India. Over time it was broadcast in fifty-five countries, although the bulk of the viewers lived in Southeast Asia.

Still another positive development for the program was that it cut across religious lines. The producers and network heads initially assumed it would be popular mainly with Hindus. Yet Muslims who lived in India, Pakistan, Malaysia, and Indonesia watched it in high numbers too. In most of these places, shortly before each new episode aired, the usually busy streets rapidly became deserted as people rushed home to watch the show. On more than one occasion, moreover, local power outages interrupted an episode in some areas. Fans were so upset that the power companies received thousands of irate complaints, including threats to burn down the power company offices if the show was not reinstated immediately.

dance performances and paintings. Of the dance presentations, among the more renowned are those in Indonesia, particularly the islands of Java and Bali. (Although a majority of Indonesians are Muslims, more than 80 percent of Bali's residents are Hindus or Buddhists, and Hinduism is one of Indonesia's six official religions.) The Sendratari Ramayana, or Ramayana Ballet, is a dance presentation still widely popular across Java. Likewise, a Balinese dance drama based on the Ramayana is routinely presented in all of Bali's Hindu temples.

Also in Indonesia, the great epic in which Rama rescues Sita from the demons who have abducted her has filtered from religion and the fine arts down into everyday life. In 1978, a group of merchants in Indonesia's capital of Jakarta (in northern Java), formed the PT Ramayana Lestari Sentosa company and built their first department store. The Ramayana stores, which today number more than seventy, sell clothes, household goods, toys, and food. Scenes from the Ramayana appear in paintings and other artistic renderings displayed in every store in the chain.

Thousands of other paintings based on the characters and events of the Ramayana were created in the past century in India, Indonesia, Malaysia, and other southern Asian countries. The largest, and perhaps most famous of these artistic depictions, was completed in 1972 by the noted Malaysian painter Syed Thajudeen. The work consists of nine large-scale panels that show three key scenes from Rama and Sita's story—Sita's abduction by the

This painting, dating from around 1810, is one of hundreds of modern artworks depicting scenes from the grand epic, the Mahabharata. In this battle scene, Krishna, one of Vishnu's several avatars, can be seen in his yellow robes at lower left.

demons, Hanuman's secret visit to Sita in the demon city of Lanka, and the burning of Lanka. This stunning artwork, which draws tourists from around the globe each year, is presently located in the National Visual Arts Gallery in Malaysia's capital, Kuala Lumpur.

Book and Film Versions of the Myths

Both the Ramayana and the Mahabharata, which together contain a large proportion of the major Hindu myths, are also the source material for numerous modern traditional novels, television series, and movies. Popular among the novels have been Pattanaik's *Sita: An Illustrated Retelling of the Ramayana*, and American animator and illustrator Sanjay Patel's *Ramayana: Divine Loophole*. In the latter work, Patel, who earlier gained acclaim for his children's book *The Little Book of Hindu Deities: From the Goddess of Wealth to the Sacred Cow*, retells Rama's heroic adventures in a brisk, lighthearted style.

Perhaps the most popular and well reviewed of all the recent written retellings of the Ramayana have been those in a series of fiction books by Indian columnist and novelist Amish Tripathi. His trilogy of books about Rama, Sita, Hanuman, and their exploits was published between 2015 and 2019. Titled *Ram: Scion of Ishkvaku*, *Sita: Warrior of Mithila*, and *Raavan: Enemy of Aryayarta*, each book in the trilogy sold more than 5 million copies in India alone. It was the second-fastest-selling book series in Indian publishing history. The only series that surpassed it was Tripathi's earlier mythological trilogy about the god Shiva. Its three novels—*The Immortals of Meluha*, *The Secret of the Nagas*, and *The Oath of the Vayuutras*—also each sold more than 5 million copies in India.

AMISH TRIPATHI
An Indian columnist and novelist who wrote a trilogy of books about the adventures of Rama

The many myths contained in the Ramayana reached even larger audiences in India and neighboring lands through a series

Ram Mohun Roy the Myth Teller

Ram Mohun Roy (1772–1833) was an Indian social and religious reformer who has often been called the father of modern India. Born in West Bengal (in eastern India), he received an extensive education and became fluent in Sanskrit, Persian, Hebrew, Arabic, and Greek by his early twenties. In 1804 he joined the East India Company, in which he served as a minor official. He retired a decade later and soon afterward settled in Calcutta. There, he began writing about religion and social customs and often called for Hindus to adopt modern ideas and practices comparable to those then shaping western Europe and America. That included the idea of Hindus commingling with Westerners, including Christians, in hopes that each culture could learn from the other. To that end, he sometimes retold the Hindu myths for both Indian and Western audiences. His versions retained the original characters, events, and concepts. But he carefully updated them, using language and situations that made them more accessible to modern readers, including, he hoped, Westerners. Among these myth-related writings were explanations of the contents of the Vedas, including descriptions of the major Hindu gods and their deeds.

of more than two dozen movies and television programs beginning in the 1950s. The very first entry, released in 1958, was both ambitious and spectacular. Titled *Sampoorna Ramayanam (The Complete Ramayana)*, the production stuck close to Valmiki's traditional version. The movie ran in theaters for 264 consecutive days, breaking Indian box office records at the time. Indian-made feature films with the same or similar titles, were released in 1961, 1963, and 1971. *Kanchana Sita*, a movie that focused more on Sita's personal experiences in the myths, was made in Malaysia in 1977.

Next came a widely popular animated Indian-Japanese film, *The Legend of Prince Rama*, in 1992. Four more animated versions of the Ramayana, or parts of it, followed; they included *Sita Sings the Blues* (2008), *Lava Kusa: The Warrior Twins* (2010), *Ramayana: The Epic* (2010), and the Thai film *Yak: The Giant King* (2012).

The television productions of these myths also reached millions of viewers. An incredible 82 percent of India's population—then over 700 million—watched the lavish 1987 television production *Ramayan*, produced and directed by Ramanand Sagar. India's Zee TV network financed and broadcast a newer version of the epic in 2002. Other notable television productions focused on the monkey god Hanuman's adventures, and one brief series that aired between 2006 and 2008 told how the demon king, Ravana, rose to power in Lanka and later died at Rama's hands. A new generation of viewers became hooked on these myths after watching the 2019 series *Ram Siya Ke Luv Kush*, which was about the adventures of Rama and Sita's twin sons, Lava and Kusha.

A Fantastically Complex Plot

The Mahabharata, which contains even more myths, both large and small, than the Ramayana, also spawned numerous works of art, comics, novels, movies, and television productions. For instance, between 2012 and 2014 Singapore-based Indian writer Krishna Udayasankar published *The Aryavarta Chronicles*, a

HASTINAPURA
The legendary kingdom around which much of the action revolves in the epic Mahabharata

series of novels based on the Mahabharata. Udayasankar skillfully dramatized and fleshed out the core story line from the original epic, which follows the *Game of Thrones*–like struggle for control of the ancient Indian kingdom of Hastinapura. The powerful Kuru clan initially holds sway, but over time it must fend off challenges by rival branches of the family. The fantastically complex plot culminates in the enormous battle of Kurukshetra, in which the Pandava family defeats the Kuru clan. Vishnu's famous avatar Krishna and other divine beings play major or minor roles, and the grand story line ends with Krishna's death.

These same events were ably dramatized and beautifully illustrated in the Amar Chitra Katha comic book version of the Mahabharata as well as in the many film versions of that huge collection of myths. Scenes from the epic appeared in various Indian films as early as 1920. Thereafter, many Indian and other southern Asian film producers and companies tackled parts or all of the complicated epic. Movie versions of parts or all of it have appeared at various times between 1932 and 2019.

Of these, the longest and most spectacular was the 1989 version, *Mahabharat*, a project guided by legendary English stage and film director Peter Brook. He first presented it on stage in a play lasting nine hours. A few months later he released the film version, which was initially nearly six hours long. (A three-hour version was released later.) One critic remarked that Brook's play and film "did nothing less than attempt to transform Hindu myth into universalized art, accessible to any culture."[31]

PETER BROOK
An English director who presented a nine-hour stage version of the Mahabharat in 1989

In a Galaxy Far, Far Away

Brook was neither the first nor the last non-Asian artist to interpret the Hindu myths and their themes for European, American, and other Western audiences. What made his version unusual in that respect was that he presented most of the characters and events of the original myths in fair detail. He made little or no attempt to water them down or explain them to Western playgoers and filmgoers, the vast majority of whom are unfamiliar with them.

Because of that unfamiliarity in the West with Hindu stories, gods, and heroes, most European and American storytellers have used a less literal approach. Instead of just retelling the original myths, they have extracted basic character types, themes, and political or social situations and have transferred these elements

One of the many posters for Return of the Jedi *shows the main characters. The creator of the* Star Wars *series, George Lucas, based those characters and much of the plot on the epic Ramayana. In this parallel, Rama became Luke Skywalker.*

to new settings and story lines. One result of this approach is that audiences are most often unaware that the material was based on Hindu mythology.

The most famous example of this Western utilization of Hindu mythical themes is producer-director George Lucas's monumental series of *Star Wars* films. (The series also includes the extensive array of novels, animated films, comic books, and video games spun off from the films). Back in the 1970s, when he first envisioned the initial three films, Lucas was strongly influenced by the Ramayana. He was certain that taking its basic story of a handsome young hero rescuing a princess from an evil villain and placing it in space in a "galaxy far, far away" would appeal strongly to American and other Western moviegoers. He also borrowed the Hindu idea of an overriding higher universal spirit (the *ishvara*). Calling it "the force," he had his characters strive to tap into and become one with it. On the many parallels between the original myths and Lucas's films, science fiction writer Damien Walter comments,

> Both stories contain the same archetypal characters, a young hero-prince in Rama/Luke, a virtuous princess who must be rescued in Sita/Leia, a morally ambiguous but loyal friend in Hanuman/Han Solo, and a master and servant of evil in Ravana/the Emperor and Indrajit/Darth Vader. Both stories are set in a fairy tale time long before the time of their audience.[32]

Stories Still Alive and Vibrant

Science fiction and outer space again proved to be apt vehicles for retelling Hindu mythological themes in director Christopher Nolan's big-budget 2014 film *Interstellar*. It starred award-winning actor Matthew McConaughey as an American astronaut who passes through various alternate dimensions in which time is bendable. Just as the Hindu deities Brahman and Vishnu repeatedly manipulate time while endlessly creating new universes, the astronaut discovers that time is not simple and moving like an arrow in one direction. Rather, it is fluid and cyclic. Therefore, what happens today already happened in the past and will happen again in the future. According to Indian journalist Nirpal Dhaliwal,

> When the film's astronaut hero declares that the mysterious and all-knowing "they" who created a wormhole near Saturn, through which he travels to save mankind . . . are in fact "us," he is simply repeating the central notion of the Upanishads, India's oldest philosophical texts. These hold that individual human minds are merely brief reflections within a cosmic one. . . . The multi-dimensional [situation the hero] finds himself in as he comes to this realization, and in which he views life from every perspective, is the film's expression of "Indra's net," the Hindu metaphor which depicts the universe as an eternal web of existence spun by the king of the gods, each of its intersections [continually] reflecting the others.[33]

These and other cosmic concepts and gods that permeate Hindu mythology are not quaint old ideas revisited today merely because they are entertaining. For Hindus, they are living, vibrant, widely accepted elements of their dearly held belief system. Considering that, noted Indian novelist Anand Neelakantan suggests that perhaps people should stop calling them *myths*. "I was born in a place where mythology and temple arts [are] still living traditions," he points out.

So, I don't draw parallels with Greek or [Norse] cultures because their [mythologies] are stories that have stopped growing and people can't relate to the same [as in the past]. Ours is a story that has kept reinventing itself with every generation using TV serials and movies and [other art forms]. . . . The term mythology itself is misleading. If anything, they are *living* stories.[34]

SOURCE NOTES

Introduction: Mighty Indra Versus the Evil Demon

1. Ralph T.H. Griffith, trans., *Rig Veda*, Book 1, Hymn 8, Internet Sacred Text Archive. www.sacred-texts.com.
2. Kisari M. Ganguli, trans., "The Story of the Killing of Vritra," MahabharataOnline.com. www.mahabharataonline.com.
3. Jayaram V, "Good and Evil in Hinduism," Hinduwebsite.com. www.hinduwebsite.com.

Chapter One: The Ancient Indians and Their Gods

4. Veronica Ions, *Indian Mythology*. New York: Peter Bedrick, 1984, p. 11.
5. Shahrukh Husain, *Demons, Gods, and Holy Men from Indian Myths and Legends*. New York: Peter Bedrick, 1987, pp. 28–29.
6. Karel Werner, *A Popular Dictionary of Hinduism*. Chicago: NTC, 1997, pp. 6–7.
7. Griffith, trans., *Rig Veda*, Book 1, Hymn 11.
8. Ions, *Indian Mythology,* p. 18.
9. Quoted in AumAmen, "Hanuman Chalisa." http://aumamen.com.
10. Barbara S. Miller, trans., *Bhagavad-Gita*. New York: Bantam, 2004, p. 35.
11. Mark Cartwright, "Hindu Architecture," *Ancient History Encyclopedia*, September 4, 2015. www.ancient.eu.
12. Gavin Flood, "History of Hinduism," BBC, August 24, 2009. www.bbc.co.uk.

Chapter Two: The Creation of the World and Humans

13. Genesis 1:3.
14. Devdutt Pattanaik, "How Did the World Come Into Being According to Hinduism?," Dailyo, September 15, 2017. www.dailyo.in.

15. Ions, *Indian Mythology*, p. 24.

16. Ions, *Indian Mythology*, p. 25.

17. Mark Cartwright, "Brahma," *Ancient History Encyclopedia*, May 16, 2015. www.ancient.eu.

18. Quoted in Husain, *Demons, Gods, and Holy Men from Indian Myths and Legends*, p. 59.

Chapter Three: Tales of Love and Lovers

19. Subhamoy Das, "Immortal Love Legends: Romantic Tales from Hindu Literature," Learn Religions, August 2, 2018. www.learnreligions.com.

20. Kavita Kane, "Rediscovering 10 Intense Love Stories from Indian Mythology," She the People, February 13, 2018. www .shethepeople.tv.

21. Shreekant Vijaykar, "The Story of Vivasvat (Surya) and San-jana (Sandhya)," *Ruminations on Hindu Mythology* (blog), October 17, 2017. http://hindumyths.blogspot.com.

22. Husain, *Demons, Gods, and Holy Men from Indian Myths and Legends*, p. 88.

Chapter Four: Stalwart Heroes Versus Foul Demons

23. Karanam N. Rao, "The Might of Bhima and the Death of Bakasura," *Uncle Katha* (blog), August 2019. https://uncle katha.com.

24. Mark Cartwright, "Rama," *Ancient History Encyclopedia*, September 13, 2015. www.ancient.eu.

25. Elizabeth Seeger, ed., *The Ramayana*. New York: William R. Scott, 1969, p. 106.

26. Seeger, ed., *The Ramayana*, p. 118.

27. Seeger, ed., *The Ramayana*, pp. 212–13.

28. Mark Cartwright, "Ravana." *Ancient History Encyclopedia*, April 13, 2016. www.ancient.eu.

Chapter Five: The Hindu Myths in Modern Culture

29. Quoted in Nitya Atmakur, "Devdutt Pattanaik on His New Book *Faith*: 'Myths Are a Necessary Part of the Human Condition, Not Just Ancient Times,'" Firstpost, April 25, 2019. www.firstpost.com.

30. Vamsee Juluri, "Mythology, Media, and the Future of Hinduism," *HuffPost*, May 25, 2011. www.huffpost.com.
31. Margaret Croyden, "Peter Brook Transforms an Indian Epic for the Stage," *New York Times*, August 25, 1985. www.nytimes.com.
32. Damien Walter, "The 3,000 Year Old Story That Inspired *Star Wars*," *Science Fiction* (blog), Medium, December 11, 2017. https://medium.com.
33. Nirpal Dhaliwal, "How Movies Embraced Hinduism (Without You Even Noticing)," *The Guardian*, December 25, 2014.
34. Quoted in Kiran Radhakrishna, "Our Mythology Is a Story That Keeps Reinventing Itself," *Business Line*, December 29, 2013. www.thehindubusinessline.com.

FOR FURTHER RESEARCH

Books

Swami Achuthananda, *The Reign of the Vedic Gods*. Self-published, Amazon Digital Services, 2018. Kindle.

Matt Clayton, *Hindu Mythology*. Self-published, Amazon Digital Services, 2018. Kindle.

Arshia Sattar and Sonali Zohra, *Ramayana: An Illustrated Retelling*. Brooklyn: Restless, 2018.

Shalu Sharma, *Hinduism for Beginners*. Self-published, Amazon Digital Services, 2016. Kindle.

Marie L. Shedlock, ed., *Eastern Stories and Legends*. Sandhurst, UK: Arbela, 2018.

Internet Sources

Art of Living, "The Symbolism of Ganesha." www.artofliving.org.

Swati Daftuar, "Ancient Mythology in Modern Avatars," *The Hindu*, March 29, 2016. www.thehindu.com.

Subhamoy Das, "10 of the Most Important Hindu Gods," Learn Religions, June 25, 2019. www.learnreligions.com.

Kisari M. Ganguli, trans., "The Story of the Killing of Vritra," MahabharataOnline.com. www.mahabharataonline.com.

Hindu Perspective (blog), "Purusharthas: The Four Great Aims of Life," March 17, 2013. https://hinduperspective.com.

Hinduwebsite.com, "Brahman: The Supreme Self." www.hinduwebsite.com.

Vamsee Juluri, "Mythology, Media and the Future of Hinduism," *HuffPost*, May 25, 2011. www.huffpost.com.

Museum of Art and Archaeology, "Seeing the Divine in Hindu Art," University of Missouri. https://maa.missouri.edu.

A. Sutherland, "Agni: Hindu God of Divine Illumination and One of the Three Supreme Deities of Vedic Lore," Ancient Pages, May 3, 2018. www.ancientpages.com.

A. Sutherland, "Saraswati—Hindu Goddess of Knowledge, Learning," Ancient Pages, December 18, 2017. www.ancient pages.com.

United Religions Initiative, "Hinduism: Basic Beliefs." https://uri .org.

Websites

History.com (www.history.com). One of the two or three best overall websites on the internet about Hinduism, History.com offers the basic facts behind Hindu gods, beliefs, sacred writings, rituals, and much more.

Religion Facts (www.religionfacts.com). In its "Hindu Rituals and Practices" section, this fulsome site contains short overviews of the principal Hindu rituals, each with a link to an article with a much longer, more detailed account.

Religious Tolerance (www.religioustolerance.org). This is a detailed website that offers an easy-to-read summary of the evolution and beliefs of Hinduism, which many experts call the world's most complex religion.

INDEX

PICTURE CREDITS

Classical historian and award-winning author Don Nardo has written numerous acclaimed volumes about ancient civilizations and peoples. They include more than a dozen overviews of the mythologies of the Sumerians, Babylonians, Egyptians, Greeks, Romans, Persians, Celts, and others. Nardo, who also composes and arranges orchestral music, lives with his wife, Christine, in Massachusetts.